HOPE DOES NOT DISAPPOINT

SPES NON CONFUNDIT

Bull of Indiction of the
Ordinary Jubilee of the Year 2025

Francis, Bishop of Rome,
Servant of the Servants of God

Foreword by Elizabeth M. Kelly

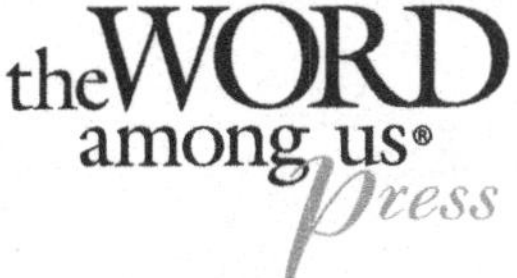

Contents

Reclaim Your Hope in Christ

Elizabeth M. Kelly

Every jubilee celebrated within the Church is a time to focus afresh on the mercy and forgiveness of God. For Jubilee Year 2025, Pope Francis has chosen to concentrate on a much-needed sub-theme taken from Paul's letter to the Romans: "Spes non confundit," or "Hope does not disappoint" (5:5).

It is a particularly bold claim for our world at this time. And a helpful reminder that Christian hope places itself on an eternal horizon. Pope Francis writes, "Christian hope does not deceive or disappoint because it is grounded in the certainty that nothing and no one may ever separate us from God's love." (See Romans 8:35: "What will separate us from the love of Christ?")

But what is hope?

Like the word "love," hope has been commandeered to refer to all kinds of things that are not true hope. For example, I can *love* chocolate and I can *love* my mother. Clearly, these "loves" are not interchangeable. The same is true for hope. I can *hope* the Vikings win the Super Bowl and I can *hope* I go to heaven. These examples of hope are not interchangeable either.

Hope, as a Christian virtue, is primarily *infused*—that is, it is a gift we are given at Baptism and through the sacraments. "Hope," writes Josef Pieper, "is the *confidently patient* expectation of eternal beatitude; . . . hope expects from God's hand the eternal life that is God himself."[1] The *Catechism* reminds us that all of the theological virtues—faith, hope and love—are *"infused by God into the souls of the faithful to make them capable* of acting as his children and of meriting eternal life. They are the pledge of the presence and action of the Holy Spirit in the faculties of the human being" (1813, emphasis mine). We must pray to the Holy Spirit for fresh infusions of hope and then cooperate and nurture those infusions when they arrive.

In this Jubilee, Pope Francis calls upon the faithful to be living signs of hope to others, making our hope palpable, especially to the sick, the imprisoned, the young, migrants, and the elderly, and that to do so, we must be a people that works for peace, has the courage to protect life at every stage, and lives joyfully. He writes:

> The Second Vatican Council says of hope that, "when people are deprived of this divine support, and lack hope in eternal life, their dignity is deeply impaired, as may so often be seen today. The problems of life and death, of guilt and suffering, remain unsolved, so that people are frequently thrown into despair." We, however, by virtue of the hope in which we

---

1   Josef Pieper, *Faith, Hope, Love* (San Francisco: Ignatius Press, 1991), 103, emphasis mine.

were saved, can view the passage of time with the certainty that the history of humanity and our own individual history are not doomed to a dead end or a dark abyss, but directed to an encounter with the Lord of glory. . . . We live our lives in expectation of his return and in the hope of living forever in him. (19)

One of the most helpful sections of *Spes non confudit* is the connection Pope Francis draws between the virtues of hope and what he calls "the daughter of hope," patience. He says:

In our fast-paced world, we are used to wanting everything now. We no longer have time simply to be with others. . . . Patience has been put to flight by frenetic haste, and this has proved detrimental, since it leads to impatience, anxiety and even gratuitous violence, resulting in more unhappiness and self-centeredness.

Nor is there much place for patience in this age of the Internet, as space and time yield to an ever-present "now." . . . Saint Paul often speaks of patience in the context of our need for perseverance and confident trust in God's promises. . . . Patience, one of the fruits of the Holy Spirit, sustains our hope and strengthens it as a virtue and a way of life. May we learn to pray frequently for the grace of patience, which is both the daughter of hope and at the same time its firm foundation. (4)

Let us strive to make the Jubilee Year 2025 a year rooted in hope, the hope of forgiveness and mercy, the hope of joy and peace, the hope of Christ.

What Is a Jubilee?

For the people of Israel, the Jubilee year was a remembrance of God's mercy in the past and a call to extend that mercy to people in the present. Every fifty years, the Jubilee was set aside to reestablish a proper relationship with God, with one another, and with all of creation. It involved the forgiveness of debts, the return of misappropriated land, and a fallow period for the fields.

Today, as members of the Church and believers in Christ, we celebrate a new Jubilee. Now our focus is the redemption that Jesus won for us. In the history of the Church, the first Jubilee was proclaimed in 1300, under Pope Boniface VIII. At first, Jubilees were celebrated every hundred years. In 1343, Pope Clement VI reduced them to every fifty years, and in 1470 Pope Paul II lowered them to every twenty-five years.

There have also been "extraordinary" Jubilee years: for example, in 1933 Pope Pius XI chose to commemorate the 1900th anniversary of the redemption, and in 2015 Pope Francis proclaimed the Year of Mercy as an Extraordinary Jubilee.

A Jubilee Year has traditionally been marked by a pilgrimage to the Roman Basilicas of St. Peter and St. Paul. It now also includes the opening of the Holy Door, as well as a special invitation to the Sacrament of Reconciliation and to prayer. Those who participate in the Jubilee are granted a plenary indulgence.

What Is a Papal Bull of Indiction?

Tradition holds that each Jubilee is proclaimed through the publication of a Papal Bull of Indiction. A "Bull" is an official document, generally written in Latin and bearing the seal (*bulla*) of the Pope, and "Indiction" is derived from the Latin *indicere*, to proclaim. Each Bull is identified by its opening words, in this case, *Spes non confudit*, "Hope does not disappoint."

To all who read this letter,
may hope fill your hearts.

Spes Non Confundit

1. *Spes non confundit.* "Hope does not disappoint" (Romans 5:5). In the spirit of hope, the Apostle Paul addressed these words of encouragement to the Christian community of Rome. Hope is also the central message of the coming Jubilee that, in accordance with an ancient tradition, the Pope proclaims every twenty-five years. My thoughts turn to all those *pilgrims of hope* who will travel to Rome in order to experience the Holy Year and to all those others who, though unable to visit the City of the Apostles Peter and Paul, will celebrate it in their local Churches. For everyone, may the Jubilee be a moment of genuine, personal encounter with the Lord Jesus, the "door" (cf. John 10:7.9) of our salvation, whom the Church is charged to proclaim always, everywhere and to all as "our hope" (1 Timothy 1:1).

Everyone knows what it is to hope. In the heart of each person, hope dwells as the desire and expectation of good things to come, despite our not knowing what the future may bring. Even so, uncertainty about the future may at times give rise

For everyone, may the Jubilee be a moment of genuine, personal encounter with the Lord Jesus.

to conflicting feelings, ranging from confident trust to appre-hensiveness, from serenity to anxiety, from firm conviction to hesitation and doubt. Often we come across people who are discouraged, pessimistic and cynical about the future, as if nothing could possibly bring them happiness. For all of us, may the Jubilee be an opportunity to be renewed in hope. God's word helps us find reasons for that hope. Taking it as our guide, let us return to the message that the Apostle Paul wished to communicate to the Christians of Rome.

A Word of Hope

2. "Since we are justified through faith, we have peace with God through our Lord Jesus Christ, through whom we have obtained access to this grace in which we stand; and we boast in our hope of sharing in the glory of God. . . . Hope does not disappoint, because God's love has been poured into our hearts through the Holy Spirit that has been given to us" (Romans 5:1-2.5). In this passage, Saint Paul gives us much to reflect upon. We know that the Letter to the Romans marked a decisive turning point in his work of evangelization. Until then, he had carried out his activity in the eastern part of the Empire, but now he turns to Rome and all that Rome meant in the eyes of the world. Before him lay a great challenge, which he took up for the sake of preaching the Gospel, which knows no barriers or confines. The Church of Rome was not founded by Paul, yet he felt impelled to hasten there in order to bring to everyone the Gospel of Jesus Christ, crucified and risen from the dead, a message of hope that fulfils the ancient promises, leads to glory and, grounded in love, does not disappoint.

H ope is born of love and based on the love springing from the pierced heart of Jesus upon the cross.

3. Hope is born of love and based on the love springing from the pierced heart of Jesus upon the cross: "For if while we were enemies, we were reconciled to God through the death of his Son, much more surely, having been reconciled, will we be saved by his life" (Romans 5:19). That life becomes manifest in our own life of faith, which begins with Baptism, develops in openness to God's grace and is enlivened by a hope constantly renewed and confirmed by the working of the Holy Spirit.

By his perennial presence in the life of the pilgrim Church, the Holy Spirit illumines all believers with the light of hope. He keeps that light burning, like an ever-burning lamp, to sustain and invigorate our lives. Christian hope does not deceive or disappoint because it is grounded in the certainty that nothing and no one may ever separate us from God's love: "Who will separate us from the love of Christ? Hardship, or distress, or persecution, or famine, or nakedness, or peril or the sword? No, in all these things we are more than conquerors through him who loved us. For I am convinced that neither death, nor life, nor angels, nor rulers, nor things present, nor things to come, nor powers, nor height, nor depth, nor anything else in all creation, will be able to separate us from the love of God in Christ Jesus our Lord" (Romans 8:35,37-39). Here we see the reason why this hope perseveres in the midst of trials: founded on faith and nurtured by charity, it enables us to press forward in life. As Saint Augustine observes: "Whatever our state of life, we cannot live without these three dispositions of the soul, namely, to believe, to hope and to love"[1]

4. Saint Paul is a realist. He knows that life has its joys and sorrows, that love is tested amid trials, and that hope can falter in the face of suffering. Even so, he can write: "We boast in our sufferings, knowing that suffering produces endurance, and endurance produces character, and character produces hope" (Romans 5:3-4). For the Apostle, trials and tribulations mark the lives of those who preach the Gospel amid incomprehension and persecution (2 Corinthians 6:3-10). Yet in those very contexts, beyond the darkness we glimpse a light: we come to realize that evangelization is sustained by the power flowing from Christ's cross and resurrection. In this way, we learn to practice a virtue closely linked to hope, namely *patience*. In our fast-paced world, we are used to wanting everything now. We no longer have time simply to be with others; even families find it hard to get together and enjoy one another's company. Patience has been put to flight by frenetic haste, and this has proved detrimental, since it leads to impatience, anxiety and even gratuitous violence, resulting in more unhappiness and self-centeredness.

Nor is there much place for patience in this age of the Internet, as space and time yield to an ever-present "now." Were we still able to contemplate creation with a sense of awe, we might better understand the importance of patience. We could appreciate the changes of the seasons and their harvests, observe the life of animals and their cycles of growth, and enjoy the clarity of vision of Saint Francis. In his *Canticle of the Creatures*, written exactly eight hundred years ago, Francis saw all creation as a great family and could call the sun his "brother" and the moon his "sister."[2] A renewed appreciation of the value of patience could only prove beneficial for ourselves and for others. Saint Paul often speaks of patience in the context of our need for perseverance and confident trust in God's promises. Yet, before all else, he testifies to God's own patience, as "the God of all patience and encouragement" (Romans 15:5). Patience, one of the fruits of the Holy Spirit, sustains our hope and strengthens it as a virtue and a way of life. May we learn to pray frequently for the grace of patience, which is both the daughter of hope and at the same time its firm foundation.

A Journey of Hope

5. This interplay of hope and patience makes us see clearly that the Christian life is a *journey* calling for *moments of greater intensity* to encourage and sustain hope as the constant companion that guides our steps towards the goal of our encounter with the Lord Jesus. I like to think that the proclamation of the first Jubilee, in the year 1300, was preceded by a journey of grace inspired by popular spirituality. How can we fail to recall the various ways by which the grace of forgiveness had been poured out upon God's holy and faithful People? We are reminded, for example, of the great "Pardon" that Saint Celestine V granted to all those who visited the Basilica of Santa Maria di Collemaggio in Aquila on the 28th and 29th days of August 1294, six years before Pope Boniface VIII instituted the Holy Year. The Church was already experiencing the grace of the Jubilee as an outpouring of divine mercy. Even earlier, in 1216, Pope Honorius III granted the plea of Saint Francis for an indulgence for all those visiting the Porziuncola on the first two days of August. The same can be said of the pil-

grimage to Santiago de Compostela: in 1222, Pope Callistus II allowed the Jubilee to be celebrated there whenever the Feast of the Apostle James fell on a Sunday. It is good that such "dispersed" celebrations of the Jubilee continue, so that the power of God's forgiveness can support and accompany communities and individuals on their pilgrim way.

Pilgrimage is of course a fundamental element of every Jubilee event. Setting out on a journey is traditionally associated with our human quest for meaning in life. A pilgrimage on foot is a great aid for rediscovering the value of silence, effort and simplicity of life. In the coming year, *pilgrims of hope* will surely travel the ancient and more modern routes in order to experience the Jubilee to the full. In Rome itself, along with the usual visits to the catacombs and the Seven Churches, other itineraries of faith will be proposed. Journeying from one country to another as if borders no longer mattered, and passing from one city to another in contemplating the beauty of creation and masterpieces of art, we learn to treasure the richness of different experiences and cultures, and are inspired to lift up that beauty, in prayer, to God, in thanksgiving for his wondrous works. The Jubilee Churches along the pilgrimage routes and in the city of Rome can serve as oases of spirituality and places of rest on the pilgrimage of faith, where we can drink from the wellsprings of hope, above all by approaching the sacrament of Reconciliation, the essential starting point of any true journey of conversion. In the particular Churches, special care should be taken to prepare priests and the faithful to celebrate the sacrament of Confession and to make it readily available in its individual form.

In a particular way, I would like to invite the faithful of the Eastern Churches, particularly those already in full communion with the Successor of Peter, to take part in this pilgrimage. They have suffered greatly, often even unto death, for their fidelity to Christ and the Church, and so they should feel themselves especially welcome in this City of Rome that is also their Mother and cherishes so many memories of their presence. The Catholic Church, enriched by their ancient liturgies and the theology and spirituality of their Fathers, monks and theologians, wants to give symbolic expression to its embrace of them and their Orthodox brothers and sisters in these times when they endure their own Way of the Cross, often forced by violence and instability to leave their homelands, their holy lands, for safer places. For them, the hope born of the knowledge that they are loved by the Church, which does not abandon them but follows them wherever they go, will make the symbolism of the Jubilee all the more powerful.

6. The Holy Year of 2025 is itself in continuity with preceding celebrations of grace. In the last Ordinary Jubilee, we crossed the threshold of two millennia from the birth of Jesus Christ. Then, on March 13, 2015, I proclaimed an Extraordinary Jubilee for the sake of making known and encouraging an encounter with the "merciful face of God,"[3] the core message of the Gospel for every man and woman of every time and place. Now the time has come for a new Jubilee, when once more the Holy Door will be flung open to invite everyone to an intense experience of the love of God that awakens in hearts the sure hope of salvation in Christ. The Holy Year will also guide our steps towards yet another fundamental

Now the time has come for a new Jubilee, when once more the Holy Door will be flung open to invite everyone to an intense experience of the love of God that awakens in hearts the sure hope of salvation in Christ.

celebration for all Christians: 2033 will mark the two thousandth anniversary of the redemption won by the passion, death and resurrection of the Lord Jesus. We are about to make a pilgrimage marked by great events, in which the grace of God precedes and accompanies his people as they press forward firm in faith, active in charity and steadfast in hope (cf. 1 Thessalonians 1:3).

Sustained by this great tradition, and certain that the Jubilee Year will be for the entire Church a lively experience of grace and hope, I hereby decree that the Holy Door of the Basilica of Saint Peter in the Vatican will be opened on December 24, 2024, thus inaugurating the Ordinary Jubilee. On the following Sunday, December 29, 2024, I will open the Holy Door of my cathedral, Saint John Lateran, which on November 9 this year will celebrate the 1700th anniversary of its dedication. Then, on January 1, 2025, the Solemnity of Mary, Mother of God, the Holy Door of the Papal Basilica of Saint Mary Major will be opened. Finally, Sunday, January 5, 2025, will mark the opening of the Holy Door of the Papal Basilica of Saint Paul Outside the Walls. These last three Holy Doors will be closed on Sunday, December 28, 2025.

I further decree that on Sunday, December 29, 2024, in every cathedral and co-cathedral, diocesan bishops are to celebrate Holy Mass as the solemn opening of the Jubilee Year, using the ritual indications that will be provided for that occasion. For celebrations in co-cathedrals, the bishop's place can be taken by a suitably designated delegate. A pilgrimage that sets out from a church chosen for the *collection* and then proceeds to the cathedral can serve to symbolize the journey of hope that, illumined by the word of God, unites all the faithful. In the course of this pilgrimage, passages from the present Document can be read, along with the announcement of the Jubilee Indulgence to be gained in accordance with the prescriptions found in the ritual indications mentioned above. The Holy Year will conclude in the particular Churches on Sunday, December 28, 2025; in the course of the year, every effort should be made to enable the People of God to participate fully in its proclamation of hope in God's grace and in the signs that attest to its efficacy.

The Ordinary Jubilee will conclude with the closing of the Holy Door in the Papal Basilica of Saint Peter in the Vatican on January 6, 2026, the Solemnity of the Epiphany of the Lord. During the Holy Year, may the light of Christian hope illumine every man and woman, as a message of God's love addressed to all! And may the Church bear faithful witness to this message in every part of the world!

Signs of Hope

7. In addition to finding hope in God's grace, we are also called to discover hope in the *signs of the times* that the Lord gives us. As the Second Vatican Council observed: "In every age, the Church has the responsibility of reading the signs of the times and interpreting them in the light of the Gospel. In this way, in language adapted to every generation, she can respond to people's persistent questions about the meaning of this present life and of the life to come, and how one is related to the other."[4] We need to recognize the immense goodness present in our world, lest we be tempted to think ourselves overwhelmed by evil and violence. The signs of the times, which include the yearning of human hearts in need of God's saving presence, ought to become signs of hope.

8. The first sign of hope should be the desire for *peace* in our world, which once more finds itself immersed in the tragedy of *war*. Heedless of the horrors of the past, humanity is confronting yet another ordeal, as many peoples are prey

May the Jubilee remind us that those who are peacemakers will be called "children of God."

to brutality and violence. What does the future hold for those peoples, who have already endured so much? How is it possible that their desperate plea for help is not motivating world leaders to resolve the numerous regional conflicts in view of their possible consequences at the global level? Is it too much to dream that arms can fall silent and cease to rain down destruction and death? May the Jubilee remind us that those who are peacemakers will be called "children of God" (Matthew 5:9). The need for peace challenges us all, and demands that concrete steps be taken. May diplomacy be tireless in its commitment to seek, with courage and creativity, every opportunity to undertake negotiations aimed at a lasting peace.

9. Looking to the future with hope also entails having enthusiasm for life and a readiness to share it. Sadly, in many situations this is lacking. A first effect of this is the *loss of the desire to transmit life*. A number of countries are experiencing an alarming *decline in the birthrate* as a result of today's frenetic pace, fears about the future, the lack of job security and adequate social policies, and social models whose agenda is dictated by the quest for profit rather than concern for relationships. In certain quarters, the tendency "to blame population growth, instead of extreme and selective consumerism on the part of some, is one way of refusing to face the [real] issues."[5]

Openness to life and responsible parenthood is the design that the Creator has implanted in the hearts and bodies of men and women, a mission that the Lord has entrusted to spouses and to their love. It is urgent that responsible legislation on the part of states be accompanied by the firm support of communities of believers and the entire civil community in all its components. For *the desire of young people to give birth to new sons and daughters* as a sign of the fruitfulness of their love ensures a future for every society. This is a matter of hope: it is born of hope and it generates hope.

Consequently, the Christian community should be at the forefront in pointing out the need for a *social covenant to support and foster hope*, one that is inclusive and not ideological, working for a future filled with the laughter of babies and children, in order to fill the empty cradles in so many parts of our world. All of us, however, need to recover the joy of living, since men and women, created in the image and likeness of God (cf. Genesis 1:26), cannot rest content with getting along one day at a time, settling for the here and now and seeking fulfilment in material realities alone. This leads to a narrow individualism and the loss of hope; it gives rise to a sadness that lodges in the heart and brings forth fruits of discontent and intolerance.

10. During the Holy Year, we are called to be tangible signs of hope for those of our brothers and sisters who experience hardships of any kind. I think of *prisoners* who, deprived of their freedom, daily feel the harshness of detention and its restrictions, lack of affection and, in more than a few cases, lack of respect for their persons. I propose that in this Jubilee Year governments undertake initiatives aimed at restoring hope; forms of amnesty or pardon meant to help individuals regain confidence in themselves and in society; and programs

of reintegration in the community, including a concrete commitment to respect for law.

This is an ancient appeal, one drawn from the word of God, whose wisdom remains ever timely. It calls for acts of clemency and liberation that enable new beginnings: "You shall hallow the fiftieth year and you shall proclaim liberty throughout the land to all its inhabitants" (Leviticus 25:10). This institution of the Mosaic law was later taken up by the prophet Isaiah: "The Lord has sent me to bring good news to the oppressed, to bind up the brokenhearted, to proclaim liberty to the captives and release to the prisoners, to proclaim the year of the Lord's favor" (Isaiah 61:1-2). Jesus made those words his own at the beginning of his ministry, presenting himself as the fulfilment of the "year of the Lord's favor" (cf. Luke 4:18-19). In every part of the world, believers, and their Pastors in particular, should be one in demanding dignified conditions for those in prison, respect for their human rights and above all the abolition of the death penalty, a provision at odds with Christian faith and one that eliminates all hope of forgiveness and rehabilitation.[6] In order to offer prisoners a concrete sign of closeness, I would myself like to open a Holy Door in a prison, as a sign inviting prisoners to look to the future with hope and a renewed sense of confidence.

11. Signs of hope should also be shown to the *sick*, at home or in hospital. Their sufferings can be allayed by the closeness and affection of those who visit them. Works of mercy are also works of hope that give rise to immense gratitude. Gratitude should likewise be shown to all those healthcare workers who,

often in precarious conditions, carry out their mission with constant care and concern for the sick and for those who are most vulnerable.

Inclusive attention should also be given to all those in particularly difficult situations, who experience their own weaknesses and limitations, especially those affected by illnesses or disabilities that severely restrict their personal independence and freedom. Care given to them is a hymn to human dignity, a song of hope that calls for the choral participation of society as a whole.

12. Signs of hope are also needed by those who are the very embodiment of hope, namely, *the young*. Sadly, they often see their dreams and aspirations frustrated. We must not disappoint them, for the future depends on their enthusiasm. It is gratifying to see the energy they demonstrate, for example, by rolling up their sleeves and volunteering to help when disasters strike and people are in need. Yet it is sad to see young people who are without hope, who face an uncertain and unpromising future, who lack employment or job security, or realistic prospects after finishing school. Without the hope that their dreams can come true, they will inevitably grow discouraged and listless. Escaping into drugs, risk-taking and the pursuit of momentary pleasure does greater harm to them in particular, since it closes them to life's beauty and richness, and can lead to depression and even self-destructive actions. For this reason, the Jubilee should inspire the Church to make greater efforts to reach out to them. With renewed passion, let us demonstrate care and concern for adolescents, students and young couples, the rising genera-

tion. Let us draw close to the young, for they are the joy and hope of the Church and of the world!

13. Signs of hope should also be present for *migrants* who leave their homelands behind in search of a better life for themselves and for their families. Their expectations must not be frustrated by prejudice and rejection. A spirit of welcome, which embraces everyone with respect for his or her dignity, should be accompanied by a sense of responsibility, lest anyone be denied the right to a dignified existence. *Exiles, displaced persons and refugees*, whom international tensions force to emigrate in order to avoid war, violence and discrimination, ought to be guaranteed security and access to employment and education, the means they need to find their place in a new social context.

May the Christian community always be prepared to defend the rights of those who are most vulnerable, opening wide its doors to welcome them, lest anyone ever be robbed of the hope of a better future. May the Lord's words in the great parable of the Last Judgement always find an echo in our hearts: "I was a stranger and you welcomed me" for "just as you did it to one of the least of these my brothers and sisters, you did it to me" (Matthew 25:35,40).

14. The *elderly*, who frequently feel lonely and abandoned, also deserve signs of hope. Esteem for the treasure that they are, their life experiences, their accumulated wisdom and the contribution that they can still make, is incumbent on the Christian community and civil society, which are called to cooperate in strengthening the covenant between generations.

Here I would also mention *grandparents*, who represent the passing on of faith and wisdom to the younger generation. May they find support in the gratitude of their children and the love of their grandchildren, who discover in them their roots and a source of understanding and encouragement.

15. I ask with all my heart that hope be granted to the billions of the *poor*, who often lack the essentials of life. Before the constant tide of new forms of impoverishment, we can easily grow inured and resigned. Yet we must not close our eyes to the dramatic situations that we now encounter all around us, not only in certain parts of the world. Each day we meet people who are poor or impoverished; they may even be our next-door neighbors. Often they are homeless or lack sufficient food for the day. They suffer from exclusion and indifference on the part of many. It is scandalous that in a world possessed of immense resources, destined largely to producing weapons, the poor continue to be "the majority of the planet's population, billions of people. These days they are mentioned in international political and economic discussions, but one often has the impression that their problems are brought up as an afterthought, a question which gets added almost out of duty or in a tangential way, if not treated merely as collateral damage. Indeed, when all is said and done, they frequently remain at the bottom of the pile."[7] Let us not forget: the poor are almost always the victims, not the ones to blame.

Appeals for Hope

16. Echoing the age-old message of the prophets, the Jubilee reminds us that *the goods of the earth* are not destined for a privileged few, but for everyone. The rich must be generous and not avert their eyes from the faces of their brothers and sisters in need. Here I think especially of those who lack water and food: hunger is a scandal, an open wound on the body of our humanity, and it summons all of us to a serious examination of conscience. I renew my appeal that "with the money spent on weapons and other military expenditures, let us establish a global fund that can finally put an end to hunger and favor development in the most impoverished countries, so that their citizens will not resort to violent or illusory situations, or have to leave their countries in order to seek a more dignified life."[8]

Another heartfelt appeal that I would make in light of the coming Jubilee is directed to the more affluent nations. I ask that they acknowledge the gravity of so many of their past decisions and determine to *forgive the debts* of countries that

All the baptized, with their respective charisms and ministries, are co-responsible for ensuring that manifold signs of hope bear witness to God's presence in the world.

will never be able to repay them. More than a question of generosity, this is a matter of justice. It is made all the more serious today by a new form of injustice which we increasingly recognize, namely, that "a true 'ecological debt' exists, particularly between the global North and South, connected to commercial imbalances with effects on the environment and the disproportionate use of natural resources by certain countries over long periods of time."[9] As sacred Scripture teaches, the earth is the Lord's and all of us dwell in it as "aliens and tenants" (Leviticus 25:23). If we really wish to prepare a path to peace in our world, let us commit ourselves to remedying the remote causes of injustice, settling unjust and unpayable debts, and feeding the hungry.

17. The coming Jubilee Year will also coincide with a significant date for all Christians, namely, *the 1700th anniversary of the celebration of the first great Ecumenical Council, that of Nicaea*. It is worth noting that, from apostolic times, bishops have gathered on various occasions in order to discuss doctrinal questions and disciplinary matters. In the first centuries of Christianity, synods frequently took place in both East and West, showing the importance of ensuring the unity of God's People and the faithful proclamation of the Gospel. The Jubilee can serve as an important occasion for giving concrete expression to this form of synodality, which the Christian community today considers increasingly necessary for responding to the urgent need for evangelization. All the baptized, with their respective charisms and ministries, are co-responsible for ensuring that manifold signs of hope bear witness to God's presence in the world.

The Council of Nicaea sought to preserve the Church's unity, which was seriously threatened by the denial of the full divinity of Jesus Christ and hence his consubstantiality with the Father. Some three hundred bishops took part, convoked at the behest of the Emperor Constantine; their first meeting took place in the Imperial Palace on May 20, 325. After various debates, by the grace of the Spirit they unanimously approved the Creed that we still recite each Sunday at the celebration of the Eucharist. The Council Fathers chose to begin that Creed by using for the first time the expression "*We believe*,"[10] as a sign that all the Churches were in communion and that all Christians professed the same faith.

The Council of Nicaea was a milestone in the Church's history. The celebration of its anniversary invites Christians to join in a hymn of praise and thanksgiving to the Blessed Trinity and in particular to Jesus Christ, the Son of God, "consubstantial with the Father,"[11] who revealed to us that mystery of love. At the same time, Nicaea represents a summons to all Churches and Ecclesial Communities to persevere on the path to visible unity and in the quest of fitting ways to respond fully to the prayer of Jesus "that they may all be one. As you, Father, are in me and I am in you, may they also be in us, so that the world may believe that you have sent me" (John 17:21).

The Council of Nicaea also discussed the date of Easter. To this day, different approaches to this question prevent celebrating the fundamental event of our faith on the same day. Providentially, a common celebration will take place in the year 2025. May this serve as an appeal to all Christians, East and West, to take a decisive step forward towards unity around a common date for Easter. We do well to remind ourselves that many people, unaware of the controversies of the past, fail to understand how divisions in this regard can continue to exist.

Anchored in Hope

18. Hope, together with faith and charity, makes up the triptych of the "theological virtues" that express the heart of the Christian life (cf. 1 Corinthians 13:13; 1 Thessalonians 1:3). In their inseparable unity, hope is the virtue that, so to speak, gives inward direction and purpose to the life of believers. For this reason, the Apostle Paul encourages us to "rejoice in hope, be patient in suffering, and persevere in prayer" (Romans 12:12). Surely we need to "abound in hope" (cf. Romans 15:13), so that we may bear credible and attractive witness to the faith and love that dwell in our hearts; that our faith may be joyful and our charity enthusiastic; and that each of us may be able to offer a smile, a small gesture of friendship, a kind look, a ready ear, a good deed, in the knowledge that, in the Spirit of Jesus, these can become, for those who receive them, rich seeds of hope. Yet what is the basis of our hope? To understand this, let us stop and reflect on "the reasons for our hope" (cf. 1 Peter 3:15).

We live our lives in expectation of Jesus' return and in the hope of living forever in him.

19. "I believe in *life everlasting*."[12] So our faith professes. Christian hope finds in these words an essential foundation. For hope is "that theological virtue by which we desire . . . eternal life as our happiness."[13] The Second Vatican Council says of hope that, "when people are deprived of this divine support, and lack hope in eternal life, their dignity is deeply impaired, as may so often be seen today. The problems of life and death, of guilt and suffering, remain unsolved, so that people are frequently thrown into despair."[14] We, however, by virtue of the hope in which we were saved, can view the passage of time with the certainty that the history of humanity and our own individual history are not doomed to a dead end or a dark abyss, but directed to an encounter with the Lord of glory. As a result, we live our lives in expectation of his return and in the hope of living forever in him. In this spirit, we make our own the heartfelt prayer of the first Christians with which sacred Scripture ends: "Come, Lord Jesus!" (Revelation 22:20).

20. The death and resurrection of Jesus is the heart of our faith and the basis of our hope. Saint Paul states this succinctly by the use of four verbs: "I handed on to you as of first importance what I in turn had received, that Christ died for our sins in accordance with the Scriptures, and that he was buried, and that he was raised on the third day in accordance with the Scriptures, and that he appeared to Cephas and then to the twelve" (1 Colossians 15:3-5). Christ *died, was buried, was raised* and *appeared*. For our sake, Jesus experienced the drama of death. The Father's love raised him in the power of the Spirit, and made of his humanity the first fruits of our

eternal salvation. Christian hope consists precisely in this: that in facing death, which appears to be the end of everything, we have the certainty that, thanks to the grace of Christ imparted to us in Baptism, "life is changed, not ended,"[15] forever. Buried with Christ in Baptism, we receive in his resurrection the gift of a new life that breaks down the walls of death, making it a passage to eternity.

The reality of *death*, as a painful separation from those dearest to us, cannot be mitigated by empty rhetoric. The Jubilee, however, offers us the opportunity to appreciate anew, and with immense gratitude, the gift of the new life that we have received in Baptism, a life capable of transfiguring death's drama. It is worth reflecting, in the context of the Jubilee, on how that mystery has been understood from the earliest centuries of the Church's life. An example would be the tradition of building baptismal fonts in the shape of an octagon, as seen in many ancient baptisteries, like that of Saint John Lateran in Rome. This was intended to symbolize that Baptism is the dawn of the "eighth day," the day of the resurrection, a day that transcends the normal, weekly passage of time, opening it to the dimension of eternity and to life everlasting: the goal to which we tend on our earthly pilgrimage (cf. Romans 6:22).

The most convincing testimony to this hope is provided by the *martyrs*. Steadfast in their faith in the risen Christ, they renounced life itself here below, rather than betray their Lord. Martyrs, as confessors of the life that knows no end, are present and numerous in every age, and perhaps even more so in our own day. We need to treasure their testimony, in order to confirm our hope and allow it to bear good fruit.

The martyrs, coming as they do from different Christian traditions, are also seeds of unity, expressions of the ecumenism of blood. I greatly hope that the Jubilee will also include ecumenical celebrations as a way of highlighting the richness of the testimony of these martyrs.

21. What, then, will become of us after death? With Jesus, beyond this threshold we will find eternal life, consisting in full communion with God as we forever contemplate and share in his infinite love. All that we now experience in hope, we shall then see in reality. We are reminded of the words of Saint Augustine: "When I am one with you in all my being, there will be no more pain and toil; my life shall be true life, a life wholly filled by you."[16] What will characterize this fullness of communion? Being happy. *Happiness* is our human vocation, a goal to which all aspire.

But what is happiness? What is the happiness that we await and desire? Not some fleeting pleasure, a momentary satisfaction that, once experienced, keeps us longing for more, in a desperate quest that leaves our hearts unsated and increasingly empty. We aspire to a happiness that is definitively found in the one thing that can bring us fulfilment, which is love. Thus, we will be able to say even now: I am loved, therefore I exist; and I will live forever in the love that does not disappoint, the love from which nothing can ever separate me. Let us listen once more to the words of the Apostle: "I am convinced that neither death, nor life, nor angels, nor rulers, nor things present, nor things to come, nor powers, nor height, nor depth, nor anything else in all creation, will be able to separate us from the love of God in Christ Jesus our Lord" (Romans 8:38-39).

22. Another reality having to do with eternal life is *God's judgement*, both at the end of our individual lives and at the end of history. Artists have often attempted to portray it—here we can think of Michelangelo's *magnum opus* in the Sistine Chapel—in accordance with the theological vision of their times and with the aim of inspiring a sense of awe in the viewer. We should indeed prepare ourselves consciously and soberly for the moment when our lives will be judged, but we must always do this from the standpoint of hope, the theological virtue that sustains our lives and shields them from groundless fear. The judgement of God, who is love (cf. 1 John 4:8,16), will surely be based on love, and in particular on all that we have done or failed to do with regard to those in need, in whose midst Christ, the Judge himself, is present (cf. Matthew 25:31-46). Clearly, then, we are speaking of a judgement unlike any handed down by human, earthly tribunals; it should be understood as a rapport of truth with the God who is love and with oneself, within the unfathomable mystery of divine mercy. Sacred Scripture states: "You have taught your people that the righteous must be kind, and you have filled your children with good hope, because you give repentance for sins, so that . . . when we are judged, we may expect mercy" (Wisdom 12:19,22). In the words of Benedict XVI: "At the moment of judgement we experience and we absorb the overwhelming power of his love over all the evil in the world and in ourselves. The pain of love becomes our salvation and our joy."[17]

Judgement, then, concerns the salvation in which we hope and which Jesus has won for us by his death and resurrection. It is meant to bring us to a definitive encounter with the Lord. The evil we have done cannot remain hidden; it needs to be *purified* in order to enable this definitive encounter with God's love. Here we begin to see the need of our prayers for all those who have ended their earthly pilgrimage, our solidarity in an intercession that is effective by virtue of the communion of the saints, and the shared bond that makes us one in Christ, the firstborn of all creation. The Jubilee indulgence, thanks to the power of prayer, is intended in a particular way for those who have gone before us, so that they may obtain full mercy.

23. Indeed, the *indulgence* is a way of discovering the unlimited nature of God's mercy. Not by chance, for the ancients, the terms "mercy" and "indulgence" were interchangeable, as expressions of the fullness of God's forgiveness, which knows no bounds.

The *sacrament of Penance* assures us that God wipes away our sins. We experience those powerful and comforting words of the Psalm: "It is he who forgives all your guilt, who heals every one of your ills, who redeems your life from the grave, who crowns you with love and compassion. . . . The Lord is compassion and love, slow to anger and rich in mercy. . . . He does not treat us according to our sins, nor repay us according to our faults. For as the heavens are high above the earth, so strong is his love for those who fear him. As far as the east is from the west, so far does he remove our sins" (Psalm 103:3-4,8,10-12). The sacrament of Reconciliation is not only a magnificent spiritual gift, but also a decisive, essential and

Let us not neglect Confession, but rediscover the beauty of this sacrament of healing and joy, the beauty of God's forgiveness of our sins!

fundamental step on our journey of faith. There, we allow the Lord to erase our sins, to heal our hearts, to raise us up, to embrace us and to reveal to us his tender and compassionate countenance. There is no better way to know God than to let him reconcile us to himself (cf. 2 Corinthians 5:20) and savor his forgiveness. Let us not neglect Confession, but rediscover the beauty of this sacrament of healing and joy, the beauty of God's forgiveness of our sins!

Still, as we know from personal experience, every sin "leaves its mark." Sin has consequences, not only outwardly in the effects of the wrong we do, but also inwardly, inasmuch as "every sin, even venial, entails an unhealthy attachment to creatures, which must be purified either here on earth, or after death, in the state called Purgatory."[18] In our humanity, weak and attracted by evil, certain residual effects of sin remain. These are removed by the indulgence, always by the grace of Christ, who, as Saint Paul VI wrote, "is himself our 'indulgence.'"[19] The Apostolic Penitentiary will issue norms for obtaining and rendering spiritually fruitful the practice of the Jubilee indulgence.

This experience of full forgiveness cannot fail to open our hearts and minds to the need to *forgive others* in turn. Forgiveness does not change the past; it cannot change what happened in the past, yet it can allow us to change the future and to live different lives, free of anger, animosity and vindictiveness. Forgiveness makes possible a brighter future, which enables us to look at the past with different eyes, now more serene, albeit still bearing the trace of past tears.

For the last Extraordinary Jubilee, I commissioned *Missionaries of Mercy*, and these continue to carry out an important mission. During the coming Jubilee, may they exercise their ministry by reviving hope and offering forgiveness whenever a sinner comes to them with an open heart and a penitent spirit. May they remain a source of reconciliation and an encouragement to look to the future with heartfelt hope inspired by the Father's mercy. I encourage bishops to take advantage of their precious ministry, especially by sending them wherever hope is sorely tested: to prisons, hospitals, and places where people's dignity is violated, poverty abounds and social decay is prevalent. In this Jubilee Year, may no one be deprived of the opportunity to receive God's forgiveness and consolation.

24. Hope finds its supreme witness in *the Mother of God*. In the Blessed Virgin, we see that hope is not naive optimism but a gift of grace amid the realities of life. Like every mother, whenever Mary looked at her Son, she thought of his future. Surely she kept pondering in her heart the words spoken to her in the Temple by the elderly Simeon: "This child is destined for the falling and rising of many in Israel, and to be a sign that will be opposed, so that the inner thoughts of many will be revealed—and a sword will pierce your own soul too" (Luke 2:34-35). At the foot of the cross, she witnessed the passion and death of Jesus, her innocent son. Overwhelmed with grief, she nonetheless renewed her "fiat," never abandoning her hope and trust in God. In this way, Mary cooperated for our sake in the fulfilment of all that her Son had foretold in announcing that he would have to "undergo great suffering, and be rejected by the elders, the chief priests, and the scribes,

and be killed, and after three days rise again" (Mark 8:31). In the travail of that sorrow, offered in love, Mary became our Mother, the Mother of Hope. It is not by chance that popular piety continues to invoke the Blessed Virgin as *Stella Maris*, a title that bespeaks the sure hope that, amid the tempests of this life, the Mother of God comes to our aid, sustains us and encourages us to persevere in hope and trust.

In this regard, I would note that the Shrine of Our Lady of Guadalupe in Mexico City is preparing to celebrate, in 2031, the fifth centenary of Our Lady's first apparition. Through Juan Diego, the Mother of God brought a revolutionary message of hope that she continues to bring to every pilgrim and all the faithful: "Am I not here, who am your Mother?"[20] That message continues to touch hearts in the many Marian shrines throughout the world, where countless pilgrims commend to the holy Mother of God their cares, their sorrows and their hopes. During the Jubilee Year, may these shrines be sacred places of welcome and privileged spaces for the rebirth of hope. I encourage all pilgrims to Rome to spend time in prayer in the Marian shrines of the City, in order to venerate the Blessed Mother and to implore her protection. I am confident that everyone, especially the suffering and those most in need, will come to know the closeness of Mary, the most affectionate of mothers, who never abandons her children and who, for the holy people of God, is "a sign of certain hope and comfort."[21]

25. In our journey towards the Jubilee, let us return to Scripture and realize that it speaks to us in these words: "May we who have taken refuge in him be strongly encouraged to seize

the hope set before us. We have this hope, a sure and steadfast anchor of the soul, a hope that enters the inner shrine behind the curtain, where Jesus, a forerunner on our behalf, has entered" (Hebrews 6:18-20). Those words are a forceful encouragement for us never to lose the hope we have been given, to hold fast to that hope and to find in God our refuge and our strength.

The image of the anchor is eloquent; it helps us to recognize the stability and security that is ours amid the troubled waters of this life, provided we entrust ourselves to the Lord Jesus. The storms that buffet us will never prevail, for we are firmly anchored in the hope born of grace, which enables us to live in Christ and to overcome sin, fear and death. This hope, which transcends life's fleeting pleasures and the achievement of our immediate goals, makes us rise above our trials and difficulties, and inspires us to keep pressing forward, never losing sight of the grandeur of the heavenly goal to which we have been called.

The coming Jubilee will thus be a Holy Year marked by the hope that does not fade, our hope in God. May it help us to recover the confident trust that we require, in the Church and in society, in our interpersonal relationships, in international relations, and in our task of promoting the dignity of all persons and respect for God's gift of creation. May the witness of believers be for our world a leaven of authentic hope, a harbinger of new heavens and a new earth (2 Peter 3:13), where men and women will dwell in justice and harmony, in joyful expectation of the fulfilment of the Lord's promises.

Let us even now be drawn to this hope! Through our witness, may hope spread to all those who anxiously seek it. May the way we live our lives say to them in so many words: "Hope in the Lord! Hold firm, take heart and hope in the Lord!" (Psalm 27:14). May the power of hope fill our days, as we await with confidence the coming of the Lord Jesus Christ, to whom be praise and glory, now and forever.

Given in Rome, at Saint John Lateran, on May 9, the Solemnity of the Ascension of our Lord Jesus Christ, in the year 2024, the twelfth of my Pontificate.

Francis

Notes

[1] *Serm.* 198 augm. 2.

[2] Cf. *Fonti Francescane*, No. 263, 6.10.

[3] Cf. Bull of Indiction of the Extraordinary Jubilee of Mercy *Misericordiae Vultus*, 1-3.

[4] Pastoral Constitution *Gaudium et Spes*, 4.

[5] Encyclical Letter *Laudato Si'*, 50.

[6] Cf. *Catechism of the Catholic Church*, No. 2267.

[7] Encyclical Letter *Laudato Si'*, 49.

[8] Encyclical Letter *Fratelli Tutti*, 262.

[9] Encyclical Letter *Laudato Si'*, 51.

[10] Nicene Creed: H. Denzinger-A. Schönmetzer, *Enchiridion symbolorum definitionum et declarationum de rebus fidei et morum*, 125.

[11] Ibid.

[12] Apostles' Creed: H. Denzinger-A. Schönmetzer, *Enchiridion symbolorum definitionum et declarationum de rebus fidei et morum*, 30.

[13] *Catechism of the Catholic Church*, No. 1817.

[14] Pastoral Constitution *Gaudium et Spes*, 21.

[15] Roman Missal, *Preface I for the Dead*.

[16] *Confessions*, X, 28.

[17] Encyclical Letter *Spe Salvi*, 47.

[18] *Catechism of the Catholic Church*, No. 1472.

[19] Apostolic Letter *Apostolorum Limina*, 23 May 1974, II.

[20] *Nican Mopohua*, No. 119.

[21] Second Vatican Ecumenical Council, Dogmatic Constitution *Lumen Gentium*, 68.

Made in the USA
Coppell, TX
19 January 2025

44630609R00036